101 Ways

to get a

Good
Night's
Sleep

This edition published in 2017
by Baker & Taylor UK Ltd
Bicester, Oxfordshire OX26 4ST

© Susanna Geoghegan Gift Publishing

Author: Michael Powell

Cover design: Milestone Creative

Contents layout: Seagulls

ISBN: 978-1-911517-09-2

Printed in China

GOOD NIGHT'S SLEEP

From vitamins to room temperature and modern communications technology to gut bacteria, dozens of variables work together to ensure you get a good night's sleep. Just one or two of them need be out of whack for you to join the ten per cent of the population that suffers from a sleep disorder.

Fortunately there are scores of tools available to help you explore the roots of the problem and improve your sleeping habits. Most of them fall into one of four important categories: routine, diet, your mental approach and intricate biochemistry.

Even if you appear to have no trouble sleeping, this book may reveal sleeping routines that are far from healthy. Everyone can benefit from following this advice to gain more energy, a beefed-up immune system, greater clarity of thought and a better quality of life.

★ GET THE CONDITIONS RIGHT ★

It's important to create an environment that is conducive to quality sleep and there are many factors to consider. First, make sure the room is dark, cool (18°C/65°F with about 65 per cent humidity – see page 19) and quiet. Any light, but especially blue light, disrupts sleeping patterns, so try to reduce your exposure to bright artificial lights (including screens) for an hour before bedtime. Keep your bedroom clean and tidy, as a messy room can also disturb your sleep (those who surround themselves with extreme clutter often report trouble sleeping). Finally stick to bedroom activities (e.g. don't work, eat or perform vigorous exercise in your bedroom). If possible, relocate 'daytime' items like your desk, printer, cross-trainer, television, filing cabinet – anything you associate with activity and business, rather than restfulness.

Never waste any time you can spend sleeping.

FRANK H. KNIGHT

Oh! lightly, lightly tread!
A holy thing is sleep,
On the worn spirit shed,
And eyes that wake to weep.

FELICIA HEMANS, *THE SLEEPER*

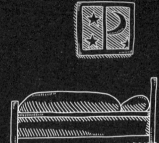

★ EAT FOODS THAT CONTAIN TRYPTOPHAN ★

Tryptophan is an essential amino acid that is used in the biosynthesis of proteins. It is called 'essential' because humans cannot create it inside their bodies, so they can only get it from their diet. If you were to completely eliminate tryptophan from your diet, you would become ill and eventually die. It is also vital for psychological health and sleep, is involved in the production of melatonin (which helps control your sleep and wake cycles) and is a precursor for the production of serotonin, an important neurotransmitter which promotes feelings of wellbeing and happiness as well as regulating appetite and sleep. The best dietary sources in order of concentration are dried egg whites, fish, cheese, chia seeds, sesame seeds, sunflower seeds, tofu, meat, raw oats and milk. Bananas are often cited as a good source, but all these other foods have higher levels.

★ ESTABLISH A RESTFUL PRE-SLEEP ROUTINE ★

Our bodies are regulated by a 24-hour clock called the circadian rhythm, which involves delicate biochemistry: the release or suppression of hormones and mood-altering chemicals at specific times during the day and night. Work with it by giving your body a predictable night-time routine: eat your final meal of the day at a similar time (try to avoid eating after 8pm), perform the same winding-down activities that work for you, and go to sleep at the same time every night, when you are ready to sleep, and early enough so that you can wake naturally without relying on your alarm clock. Your bedtime routine needn't be long: just twenty minutes of restful preparation every evening can have a profound effect on the quality of your sleep.

A tiger only needs three things to be comfortable. Lots of food, sleep, and ... actually, no, it's just those two things.

COLLEEN HOUCK

★ DON'T TRY AND FORCE YOURSELF TO SLEEP ★

When it's three o'clock in the morning and you still can't sleep and you're panicking because you have a really busy day tomorrow and you absolutely HAVE to get to sleep NOW, change your mindset. First, acknowledge that your problems and worries seem massive at this time of night, so if your problems are stopping you from sleeping, not only are they smaller than they appear right now, but you are going to have to just PARK them for a few hours so you can get some sleep ... or not. Then, accept that being awake is not the huge disaster that you think it is. Your mind and body won't disintegrate tomorrow if you don't sleep right now. Give yourself permission NOT to sleep. Get out of bed and do something else. Allow yourself the possibility of sleeping but stop chasing sleep as if your life depended on it. Your body will sleep when it needs to. Relax. Don't try to sleep, just enjoy doing nothing. Sleep may follow.

★ DON'T STAY UP PAST 11PM ★

Go to bed by 11pm whenever possible because your body creates a surge of the stress hormone cortisol after 11pm to keep you awake. That's why you can feel dog tired and ready to hit the sack and then suddenly get a second wind. Cortisol increases sugar (glucose) in the bloodstream and enhances your brain's use of sugar, neither of which are conducive to falling asleep.

Even a soul submerged in sleep is hard at work and helps make something of the world.

HERACLITUS

★ AVOID SOCIAL MEDIA FOR YOUR FIRST WAKING HOUR ★

There's no better way to ruin the benefits of a restful night's sleep than filling your head with social media as soon as you wake up. Also, turning on the radio or television to be bombarded with breaking bad news makes it harder to achieve a calm and productive morning. Studies show that people who take a week-long break from social media sites report feeling happier with life and score their wellbeing as higher. So if you aren't going to kick the habit completely, at least give yourself an hour of calm as you mentally prepare for the day. You have all day to get connected, so make the first hour an oasis of unplugged contemplation.

★ BUY A NEW MATTRESS ★

If you are in your seventies or beyond, you may rather fatalistically muse, 'people my age don't buy new beds'; alternatively, if you are very young, you may feel equally comfortable kipping on a friend's sofa as on a state-of-the-art mattress, an expense you can well do without. Optimally you should be changing your mattress once every seven to ten years (depending on its durability). Whether you choose a traditional pocket-sprung mattress (springs are sewn into individual fabric pockets) or a modern latex/memory foam model, test drive several by lying on each one for several minutes. A mattress should be soft enough to sink into, but also firm enough to support you properly, so that you feel comfortable in any position (although the best position is on your side with your knees bent).

You are the *biggest enemy* of your own sleep.

PAWAN MISHRA

★ BUY A NEW PILLOW ★

If you suffer from neck and shoulder pain in bed, wake up with a headache or pins and needles, or you just can't get comfortable, it may be the fault of your pillow. You should change your pillow at least every five years, and usually sooner. If you sleep on your front, choose a soft, thin pillow, otherwise your head will get pushed too far back. Choose a medium thickness pillow if you sleep on your back, and a medium or high support/thickness pillow if you're a side-sleeper. Whatever your sleeping position, a pillow should fully support your head so that it remains in the correct alignment with shoulders and spine as if you were standing upright. Spend as much as you can afford, because you get what you pay for and you will spend a third of your lifetime with your head on a pillow, so it's worth investing in your health and wellbeing.

> *Put my head under my pillow, and let the quiet put things where they are supposed to be.*
>
> STEPHEN CHBOSKY

★ SLEEPING PROPERLY HELPS YOU STAY SLIM ★

Many people don't have any trouble getting to sleep or staying asleep, but they do have a significant sleeping problem because their lack of a sleeping routine means that they live with and tolerate a sleep deficit, which is detrimental to physical and mental health. If you need an incentive to develop a sleeping routine, there is a strong link between lack of sleep and obesity, backed up by several scientific studies. Have you noticed how much hungrier you get when you're sleep deprived? There are two reasons for this: lack of sleep lowers the level of leptin, the hormone that tells you when you're full; it also raises the level of grehlin, the hormone which signals hunger. Sleep loss also lowers your body's core temperature, which encourages your body to conserve energy, leading to fatigue. When you're tired, you feel less motivated to do anything, so you are less physically active. Sleep also affects the influence of obesity genes. 'The less you sleep, the more important genetic factors are to how much you weigh,' says Nathaniel Watson, co-director of the University of Washington Medicine Sleep Center, in Seattle. 'The longer you sleep, the greater the influence of environmental factors like meal composition and timing.'

There is a time for many words, and there is also a

time for sleep.

HOMER

★ WRITE AWAY YOUR WORRIES ★

Instead of spending the early hours mulling over your problems and your busy schedule for the next day, jot down tomorrow's tasks and the key issues that are playing on your mind. Then lock them in a drawer and tell yourself, firmly, that no amount of worrying can help you this evening, so you may as well put everything on hold and get a good night's sleep. Refreshed, you can deal with it all anew in the morning.

★ DON'T ACCEPT THAT OLD AGE MEANS POOR SLEEP ★

Our sleeping patterns often change as we age; many older people need to go to bed earlier and/or wake up much earlier than when they were younger. As you age your body produces less growth hormone, which means you enjoy less deep sleep. If you wake feeling refreshed and ready to face the day, then these superficial changes don't matter, but if you feel exhausted during the day and regularly suffer disturbed sleep at night, don't write it off as an inevitable side-effect of growing old. It is especially important for older people to get quality sleep because it improves memory and allows cells in the body to repair. Loneliness and a lack of social engagement and stimulation are common causes of insomnia in the older population, so if none of the suggestions in this book help, it may be a warning sign that you need to reach out for help and support.

In its early stages, insomnia is almost an oasis in which those who have to think or suffer darkly take refuge.

COLETTE

★ PRESS HERE! NO. 1 ★

Press your thumb or middle finger in the indent between your eyebrows where your nose meets your forehead (the Third Eye Point). Hold for one minute while keeping your eyes closed and breathing deeply. Release for thirty seconds. Repeat twice.

Some sleepers have intelligent faces even in sleep, while other faces, even intelligent ones, become very stupid in sleep and therefore ridiculous.

FYODOR DOSTOYEVSKY

Sleeping is not time wasting.

MIKE WILSON

★ BE KIND TO YOUR GUT BACTERIA ★

The bacteria in your gut are incredibly important for your health, weight, mood and quality of sleep. In addition, it is estimated that 90 per cent of the neurotransmitter serotonin – which is associated with boosting mood and contributing to wellbeing and happiness as well as regulating appetite and sleep – is manufactured in the gut. Boost healthy gut bacteria by eating a wide variety of fresh, unprocessed foods, including vegetables, legumes, beans and fruits. Avoid artificial sweeteners and products that contain high levels of sugar. Increase your intake of fibre and eat plenty of prebiotic and probiotic foods. Eat fermented foods such as live yoghurt, sauerkraut and kimchi (see page 17), but avoid these close to bedtime, as they contain tyramine, which acts as a stimulant. Eat whole grains (see page 29), which contain lots of fibre and non-digestible carbs, such as beta-glucan, and eat foods rich in polyphenols (see page 39), which include grapes, almonds and onions, which reduce inflammation and boost gut bacteria.

I love sleep. I need sleep. We all do, of course. There are those people that don't need sleep. I think they're called 'successful'.

JIM GAFFIGAN

★ EAT PROBIOTIC FOODS ★

Probiotic foods contain live bacteria that are good for you and help maintain healthy digestion, which has wide-ranging benefits from the immune system to mental health. These super-healthy foods also help you sleep. Live yoghurt that is low in sugar is one of the best sources of probiotics (mainly lactic acid bacteria and bifidobacteria). The probiotic benefits of the fermented milk drink, kefir (made by adding kefir grains to milk) are even better than yoghurt. Unpasteurised sauerkraut – finely shredded cabbage fermented by lactic acid bacteria – is probiotic and rich in fibre and vitamins. The spicy Korean side dish kimchi is also made from fermented cabbage and is highly probiotic. Finally, introduce some pickled gherkins into your diet (pickled in salted water, not vinegar). However, avoid these foods close to bedtime, as the tyramine they contain acts as a stimulant.

When I prayed for success, I forgot to ask for sound sleep and good digestion.

MASON COOLEY

★ EAT PREBIOTIC FOODS ★

Probiotic foods contain beneficial live bacteria, but they need special food called prebiotics to live on. So don't be a neglectful host. You can't invite a colony of good bacteria to stay in your gastrointestinal tract and then not feed it. This is where prebiotic foods come in. They contain the actual food that this good bacteria needs to thrive in your gut: it's fibre, but not any old fibre, although many high-fibre foods contain some prebiotic fibre too – indigestible plant material that sits in the gut for the probiotics to feast on. The best sources by weight include raw chicory root, raw Jerusalem artichoke (also a good source of iron and potassium), raw dandelion leaves (also a good source of calcium, iron and Vitamin K), raw garlic, raw leeks (about 50g daily), raw onions (cooked onions lose half their prebiotics) and raw asparagus.

How do the angels get to sleep
When the devil leaves the porch light on?

TOM WAITS

I love having a ceiling fan, although sometimes I wish he wouldn't cheer so loud when I'm trying to sleep.

JAROD KINTZ

★ GET THE ROOM TEMPERATURE RIGHT ★

The optimal condition for sleep is a temperature of 18°C/65°F. Over a 24-hour period, body temperature fluctuates independently of the surroundings, as part of the natural circadian rhythm: it peaks during the late afternoon and reaches its minimum around 5am, a few hours before waking. If your bedroom is too hot or cold you will enjoy shorter deep sleep. Studies have measured the core body temperature of insomniacs before sleep and found them to be higher than average, so if you have trouble getting to sleep, temperature could be a key factor. If you live in a hot country, keeping your bedroom at the optimal sleep temperature will rack up the price of your air-conditioning, but there are other ways to stay cool. You can buy a cooling mattress pad filled with tiny silicone tubes that keeps the bed cool at a fraction of the cost of air-con.

I used to sleep nude – until the earthquake.

ALYSSA MILANO

★ SLEEP IN THE ALTOGETHER ★

Your core body temperature has to drop before you can go to sleep. Sleeping naked allows your body to regulate its temperature more easily. If your body can't release heat because it is trapped by your nightclothes, you will find it harder to sleep. This natural cooling also reduces your cortisol levels, so you can stay in deep sleep for longer and wake up feeling refreshed and alert. Sleeping naked also keeps your sex organs cool and allows them to breathe. Your whole body benefits from better blood flow when you sleep naked, as well as from the airing it gets. By contrast, waking up clammy because you have too many nightclothes means you are more susceptible to fungal infections such as thrush or athlete's foot.

★ YOGA POSE NO. 1 ★

Lie on your back with your arms on the floor perpendicular to your torso and with your backside and closed straight legs resting flat up against a wall. Maintain this relaxing position for five minutes.

Sometimes at night I would sleep open-eyed underneath a sky dripping with stars. I was alive then.

ALBERT CAMUS

★ SET YOUR PHONE TO FLIGHT MODE ★

Put your phone and/or tablet into flight mode to prevent it from sending or receiving calls and text messages while you sleep. Even if you don't answer it, hearing a buzz or a vibrating phone in the middle of the night means your sleep has been disturbed unnecessarily.

Though sleep is called our best friend, it is a friend who often keeps us waiting!

JULES VERNE

For sleep, one needs endless depths of blackness to sink into; daylight is too shallow, it will not cover one.

ANNE MORROW LINDBERGH

★ INVEST IN BLACKOUT CURTAINS OR BLINDS ★

Darkness is essential to effective sleep. Combine blinds and thick-backed curtains to make your bedroom as dark as possible so that you can get the best quality sleep during the early part of the night. This will also help block out noises from outside. However, you don't have to block out all the light because from dawn your body uses early morning light as a cue to start waking up, raising cortisol levels and preparing you for activity (the nadir for cortisol occurs around midnight and it peaks at around 9am). The sleep hormone, melatonin, peaks around 3am and then reduces as early morning light dramatically reduces its production.

★ SWITCH YOUR MOBILE PHONE TO NIGHT SHIFT ★

A US study into the link between frequency of mobile phone use and sleep quality was published in the journal *PLOS ONE* in 2016. It tracked 635 adults for 30 days and found the median screen-time (i.e. the time the screen was on) was 3.7 minutes per hour. It also found that longer average screen-time was associated with poor sleep quality. One of the reasons is that the screen emits blue light. However, you can reduce this problem by turning on the Night Shift function (iOS: go to settings>display & brightness>Night Shift; Android: download an app such as 'Twilight' or 'Darker'). This automatically shifts the colours of your screen into the warmer end of the colour spectrum after dark.

O soft embalmer of the still midnight!
Shutting, with careful
fingers and benign,
Our gloom-pleas'd eyes,
embower'd from the light,
Enshaded in forgetfulness divine.

JOHN KEATS

It is better to sleep on things beforehand than lie awake about them afterward.

BALTASAR GRACIAN

★ RELAX! YOU'RE GETTING MORE SLEEP THAN YOU THINK ★

Research shows that insomniacs actually get far more sleep than they give themselves credit for. It's impossible to judge how long you've been asleep, because you're asleep, so inevitably the waking periods of tossing and turning become much more prominent.

★ HAVE A CANDLE-LIT SOAK IN THE BATH BEFORE BED ★

A soothing bath prepares you for sleep in several ways. The warm water relaxes your muscles and helps you empty your mind and focus solely on the pleasure of relaxing; bathing by candlelight sends sleepy signals to your brain because dimmed light means sleep time. Finally, when you get out of the bath your body temperature drops, mimicking the way your body temperature drops naturally just before you fall asleep.

★ CHRONOLOGICALLY RETRACE YOUR DAY ★

If your mind is racing as you lie in bed, enjoy doing nothing (you've earned it) as you recap everything you did during the day, from waking to the present moment. Observe the events dispassionately, as if watching a stranger (now is not the time for recriminations and regrets).

★ PUT ON YOUR SHOES ★

How you get up every morning is as important as how you prepare yourself for sleep every evening, because constructive waking is a vital component of a healthy sleeping routine. Try putting on your shoes as soon as you get out of bed in the morning, because it's hard to crawl back under the covers with your shoes on. Then drink a small glass of cool (but not icy cold) water. Now you have your shoes on plus you're on the path to proper hydration. You're already ahead of the game.

Sleep has become profoundly important. I didn't understand the value of it.

JAMIE OLIVER

Put your thoughts to sleep, do not let them cast a shadow over the moon of your heart. Let go of thinking.

JALALUDDIN RUMI

★ AVOID FOODS THAT DISTURB SLEEP ★

Eating certain foods can be a major contributor to disturbed sleep. While dairy products in general can aid sleep, strong or aged cheeses such as Parmesan, Stilton and Romano contain high levels of the amino acid tyramine, which increases alertness. Tyramine is also found in fermented foods such as sauerkraut, teriyaki sauce and soy sauce, and processed or smoked meats such as bacon, ham and pepperoni, so avoid them before bedtime; also avoid fatty foods as these are hard to digest and produce acid in the stomach (which can lead to acid reflux). High-sugar foods should also be avoided, as they will disrupt your blood sugar levels and may make you wake in the night feeling hungry. Milk chocolate has high levels of fat and even the healthier dark chocolate contains theobromine, a compound with caffeine-like effects.

Sleep helps you win at life.

AMY POEHLER

★ EAT WHOLE GRAINS ★

Eating whole grains will improve your sleep in several ways. First, they contain lots of fibre and non-digestible carbohydrates such as beta-glucan, which promote the growth of healthy bacteria in your gut (see pages 15 and 18) such as bifidobacteria, lactobacilli and bacteroidetes. The slow-release carbohydrate promotes a slow rise in insulin, which enables tryptophan to be used by the brain. This promotes release of the feel-good neurotransmitter serotonin, which helps to regulate appetite and sleep. Whole grains also contain magnesium, which is important for sleep (see page 30) and they make you feel fuller, so you are less tempted to overeat.

★ AVOID BRIGHT LIGHTS IF YOU GET UP AT NIGHT ★

If you have to get up during the night to get a drink or use the bathroom, use the minimum of light required to safely guide you. A torch with a red filter is ideal. You want to avoid white or blue light.
You can use the light from your mobile phone, but try to find a torch app that emits light at the warm end of the spectrum (red/orange).

A well spent day brings happy sleep.

★ **LEONARDO DA VINCI** ★

★ ALL-OVER BODY MASSAGE ★

Make an all-over body massage part of your daily pre-sleep routine. It improves circulation, breaks down fat deposits, keeps your skin fresh and healthy and helps to eliminate toxins from the body. You can use a scrub to exfoliate or try a body massage glove in the bath or shower. Alternatively, perform a relaxing auto-massage with a full body massage tool or roller ball glove.

★ CHECK YOUR LEVELS OF MAGNESIUM AND CALCIUM ★

Chronic insomnia is one of the main symptoms of magnesium deficiency. Studies suggest that people who are deficient in magnesium and calcium tend to wake up after a few hours of sleep and find it hard to get back to sleep again. Calcium is required to allow your body to use the amino acid tryptophan to manufacture the sleep-regulating substance melatonin (see page 5). Dietary sources of magnesium include spinach, chard, pumpkin seeds, almonds, avocado and dark chocolate. Dietary sources of calcium include dairy products, dark leafy greens, bok choy, fortified tofu, okra, broccoli, green beans and almonds.

⋆ BLINK RAPIDLY FOR SIXTY SECONDS ⋆

Each human eye has six muscles that control its movements. The main muscles in the upper eyelid that control blinking are the *orbicularis oculi* which closes the eye and the *levator palpebrae superioris* muscle which opens the eye. You widen your eyes using the superior tarsal muscle in the upper eyelid and the inferior palpebral muscle in the lower eyelid. Blinking your eyes rapidly for one minute is said to be an effective way to make you feel sleepy. It works for the same reason any exercise makes you tired – the build-up of lactic acid that causes the burning sensation in your muscles. Rapid blinking makes your eye muscles tired so that when you stop your lids feel heavy, which sends sleepy messages to your brain.

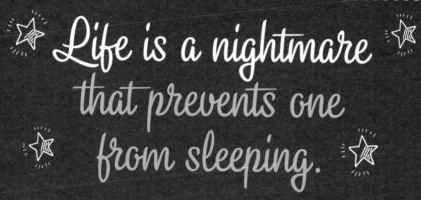

Life is a nightmare that prevents one from sleeping.

OSCAR WILDE

★ EAT HIMALAYAN SALT AND MANUKA HONEY ★

Himalayan salt is famous for its mineral content – it contains 84 minerals in total and is high in iron, magnesium, phosphorus, calcium, potassium and chloride, and also contains traces of boron, fluoride, iodine, zinc, selenium and copper, all of which are essential for good mental and physical health. Manuka honey is a monofloral honey produced in Australia and New Zealand from the nectar of the manuka tree. It's very expensive but many swear by the healing qualities of this 'liquid gold'. Honey has proven anti-inflammatory and antibacterial properties and when combined with a little Himalayan salt, it is also said to aid restful sleep. Add a pinch of the salt to a spoonful of manuka honey and then enjoy the salty-sweet mixture as you roll it around your mouth with your tongue as it gently dissolves.

We sleep, but the loom of life never stops, and the pattern which was weaving when the sun went down is weaving when it comes up in the morning.

HENRY WARD BEECHER

★ DRINK APPLE CIDER VINEGAR ★

There is lots of anecdotal evidence that a tablespoon of apple cider vinegar taken an hour before bedtime is a sleep aid; many people use it as a natural cure for acid reflux or heartburn as well as insomnia. You shouldn't drink it neat. Mix with a small mug of camomile tea and a spoonful of manuka honey. After drinking the tea, rinse your mouth with water so the vinegar doesn't sit on your tooth enamel, and wait an hour before brushing your teeth.

★ USE THE 90-MINUTE RULE ★

The typical adult sleeps about 8 hours per night, consisting of several 90-minute cycles. We feel most refreshed when we wake at the end of one of these cycles. If your alarm clock wakes you in the middle of a cycle, you will feel groggy and unrested, especially if you've been woken during a stage of deep sleep. So, work back from your wake-up time to decide the best time to go to bed. For example, if you need to wake at 7am, go to bed at either 10pm or 11.30pm.

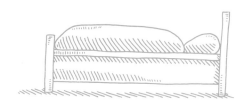

★ **SLEEP ON YOUR LEFT SIDE IF YOU ARE PREGNANT** ★

You can sleep comfortably on your back or front for the first trimester, but as the baby grows you should switch to sleeping on your side – preferably your left side. Sleeping on your back puts pressure on the aorta and the weight of your uterus pressing on your spine, back muscles and major blood vessels can inhibit blood flow to the whole body but especially to the placenta, making you feel lightheaded. Sleeping on your left side is the optimal position for blood flow to the placenta and is kindest to your heart as well as reducing pressure on the liver. Keep your legs and knees bent and place a pillow between your legs to reduce pressure on the hips and pelvis.

He never attempted to sleep on his left side, even in those dismal hours of the night when the insomniac longs for a third side after trying the two he has.

VLADIMIR NABOKOV

The best bridge between despair and hope is a good night's sleep.

E. JOSEPH COSSMAN

★ INCREASE YOUR COLLAGEN LEVELS ★

Collagen is the most abundant protein in our bodies and is the main structural protein found in skin and other connective tissues – it's the glue that holds us together. It's been described by its acolytes as a nutritional powerhouse that can improve digestive health and skin elasticity, promote weight loss, protect muscles, bones and joints and improve sleep. Levels of collagen in our body decrease with age by about 1.5 per cent a year from the age of 25. By middle age, the body loses collagen more quickly than it can be produced and by the age of sixty our collagen is cut in half. Eating lots of citrus fruit and green leafy vegetables boosts the body's natural production of collagen, while its main dietary sources are foods that are very high in protein, including beef, chicken, fish and egg whites. Better still, drink a collagen-rich broth made by boiling animal bones such as chicken feet. Collagen supplements are also available in powered form or by injection.

Sleep is more than a creature comfort. It is a requirement for life on this planet.

KAT DUFF

★ PRETEND YOU'RE DOG TIRED ★

If beating insomnia was just a matter of pretending, you think you'd have tried it years ago, but this method isn't as stupid as it sounds. Professional actors use a technique called 'sense memory', which involves recalling in vivid detail the sights, sounds, smells, taste and touch associated with a particular event in order to unlock an emotional reaction. Lie in bed and try to remember an occasion when you collapsed into bed feeling totally exhausted. Imagine yourself back on that night and conjure up the physical sensations. These might include heavy limbs, tingling legs, a slightly raw feeling inside your lungs, aching feet, etc. Make the noises you would make if you were lying down after ten hours of physical activity – contented sighs and 'ahhhs'. There are lots more examples. If your mind can remember them, so can your body, and more importantly, you'll be enjoying the feeling of relaxing after an exhausting day rather than willing yourself to sleep.

★ WEAR SOCKS (AND EVEN GLOVES) TO BED ★

Researchers from a Swiss study published in the journal *Nature* in September 1999 ('Physiology: Warm feet promote the rapid onset of sleep') demonstrated 'that the degree of dilation of blood vessels in the skin of the hands and feet, which increases heat loss at these extremities, is the best physiological predictor for the rapid onset of sleep'. In other words, the greater the vasodilatation in the hands and feet, the shorter the time it takes to fall asleep. Heating your extremities widens the blood vessels on the surface of the skin in these areas, increasing heat loss in the rest of the body, cooling it down and preparing you for sleep.

I think it is good that books still exist, but they do make me sleepy.

FRANK ZAPPA

★ DETOX WITH ACTIVATED COCONUT CHARCOAL ★

Toxins inside the body and especially inside your digestive system can wreak havoc on your circadian rhythm. Also, if your sleep cycle is out of shape, your gut bacteria will disintegrate and emit toxins as they rot and die, which further adds to the problem in a vicious circle. Occasionally ingesting activated coconut charcoal two hours before a meal is an effective way to capture harmful toxins and eliminate them from the body. The charcoal has thousands of tiny pores which literally trap the toxins. Coconut charcoal is a fine, black powder made from coconut shells that is odourless and tasteless. You can buy it from health food shops in capsule form but don't take charcoal with any other medicine and check with a doctor or medical professional first.

> I think people want very much to simplify their lives enough so that they can control the things that make it possible to sleep at night.
>
> TWYLA THARP

I studied, I met with medical doctors, scientists, and I'm here to tell you that the way to a more productive, more inspired, more joyful life is: getting enough sleep.

ARIANNA HUFFINGTON

★ EAT FOODS RICH IN POLYPHENOLS ★

Hardly a day goes by without some new obscure berry, nut or gnarly-looking vegetable being hailed as the next 'superfood', but when it comes to polyphenols, the proven health benefits are no short-term fad. Polyphenols are a group of plant-based chemicals that encompass phenolic acids, flavonoids, resveratrol, stilbenes, curcumin and lignans. Numerous studies show that they lower cholesterol and blood pressure, improve artery function and flexibility, prevent platelet clumping, boost the immune system, reduce inflammation, oxidative stress and the risks of a wide variety of cancers, increase life span and improve sleep. The top ten richest dietary sources of polyphenols by weight are cloves, star anise, cocoa powder, Mexican oregano, celery seed, black chokeberry, dark chocolate, flaxseed meal, black elderberry and chestnut.

Life is grace. Sleep is forgiveness. The night absolves. Darkness wipes the slate clean, not spotless to be sure, but clean enough for another day's chalking.

FREDERICK BUECHNER

★ BE CONSISTENT ★

The best way to improve your energy levels during the day is to establish routines that support a good night's sleep. Your body clock hates inconsistency and it loves predictability. Think of your circadian rhythm like a beloved old pet that thrives on habits. Going to bed at the same time every night can have a dramatic impact on the quality of your sleep. Don't dismiss routines as boring and lacking in spontaneity; they actually allow you to make the most of your waking life, improving your productivity, wellbeing, health and longevity and boosting your immune system.

★ AVOID ALCOHOL ★

If you rely on a nightcap to get you off to sleep, or you're a habitual drinker, you are probably suffering from impaired sleep. Alcohol reduces the time it takes to get to sleep and it appears to increase the slow wave sleep (SWS) during the first part of the night. This type of sleep is associated with healing and regeneration of bones, muscles and tissue. However, alcohol also reduces the deeper REM sleep that occurs later in the sleep cycle, during which we dream and the brain processes memories and exercises important neural connections that are vital for mental wellbeing and overall health. Lab experiments have shown a significant reduction in the lifespans of rats that were deprived of REM sleep. Alcohol consumption makes you wake earlier and your sleep may be further compromised by trips to the toilet or feeling thirsty.

A ruffled mind makes a restless pillow.

CHARLOTTE BRONTË

★ STOP SMOKING ★

Nicotine is a stimulant. Its consumption is linked to reduced deep sleep and suppressed REM sleep as well as difficulty falling and staying asleep. So people who smoke are not getting restful sleep and many suffer from diminished levels of alertness during the day. Smoking before bedtime can make it harder to fall asleep and can disrupt sleep quality: smokers spend more time in light sleep than non-smokers. Nicotine withdrawal while you sleep can also make you wake up earlier than you should, craving the first cigarette of the day. Quitting smoking will dramatically improve the quality of your sleep, but you should be aware that sleep disturbances are a common side-effect of nicotine withdrawal. Hang in there, as the positive results are worth the temporary sleep disruption.

Good night – may you fall asleep in the arms of a dream so beautiful, you'll cry when you awake.

MICHAEL FAUDET

★ CHANGE YOUR BRAIN WAVES WITH BINAURAL BEATS ★

A binaural beat is an auditory illusion created by our brains when we are played two pure-tone sine waves below 1500Hz, one in each ear, that differ in frequency by less than 40Hz. The listener hears a third tone, which is the result of their brain trying to resolve the difference. The phenomenon is believed to alter brain waves and to guide the mind into various states of consciousness, such as relaxed alertness, or sleepiness. Search YouTube for 'binaural beats sleep' and choose from hundreds of free binaural sleep aids. All you need is a pair of headphones. When you are in deep sleep, your brain generates low-frequency 'delta' waves, so these musical compositions typically focus on this end of the aural spectrum.

★ PRESS HERE! NO. 2 ★

Sit comfortably with both feet flat on the floor. Lift your left foot and place it on your right knee. Locate the talus bone (between the heel bone and the two bones of the lower leg – known as acupressure point K6) and press firmly with your right thumb for one minute while keeping your eyes closed and breathing deeply.
Release for thirty seconds.
Repeat twice, then switch legs.

The breeze at dawn has secrets to tell you. Don't go back to sleep.

JALALUDDIN RUMI

★ THE 4-7-8 TECHNIQUE ★

Invented by Harvard-trained celebrity doctor and teacher of integrative medicine, Andrew Weil, the 4-7-8 technique combines acupressure and breathing to control the parasympathetic nervous system. It's simple, safe and easy to learn. First, lightly press the tip of your tongue against the gum ridge of your top front teeth and exhale completely. Then breathe in through your nose as you count to four; hold your breath for a count of seven, then make an 'O' shape with your lips and blow out for a count of eight making a loud whooshing noise. Repeat for two minutes, focusing solely on your breathing and the silent counting. This technique increases oxygen levels in the bloodstream and helps to block distracting thoughts, allowing a feeling of calm to develop.

★ DON'T RELY ON CATCHING UP AT THE WEEKEND ★

Having a sleeping routine – going to bed and getting up at the same time every day – is preferable by far to stacking up sleep debt during the week and then trying to catch up with extra sleep at the weekend. It can take several nights of regular sleep to get you back on track after just one bad night, but the cumulative effects are much worse if you regularly borrow from the sleep bank. You'll spend several days a week feeling out of sorts until sub-par mental and physical performance becomes your accepted level of functioning, which you quickly accept as an inevitable factor of modern living. In reality, you're setting yourself up for years of feeling abnormal, with potential long-term consequences including heart disease, obesity and insulin resistance.

> *There is only one thing people like that is good for them; a good night's sleep.*

E. W. HOWE

★ TRY CATNIP! ★

Catnip (*Nepeta cataria*) is a short-lived herbaceous perennial and member of the mint family. It famously sends about 75 per cent of cats into a blissful frenzy, but did you know that it has a sedative effect on humans? Humans have used catnip medicinally for hundreds of years. The Romans used it in recipes and medicines, it was also widely used during the Middle Ages (when it was known as 'nep') and catnip tea was popular in Europe before the arrival of the Chinese tea trade. The active ingredient is nepetalactone (which also repels cockroaches, mosquitoes and rats!). You can buy catnip tea in most health food shops. Try a cup half an hour before you go to bed.

There is no sunrise so beautiful that it is worth waking me up to see it.

MINDY KALING

A flock of sheep that leisurely pass by one after one; the sound of rain, and bees murmuring; the fall of rivers, winds and seas, smooth fields, white sheets of water, and pure sky – I've thought of all by turns, and still I lie sleepless ...

WILLIAM WORDSWORTH

★ BORE YOURSELF TO SLEEP ★

Michael Breus, Clinical Psychologist and Author of *Good Sleep* counts backwards from 300 by threes to help him get to sleep: 'It is mathematically so complicated you can't think of anything else, and it is so boring I am out like a light!' Whatever variation of 'counting sheep' you choose, from visualising a waterfall or walk on a beach to calculating the cube root of six-figure numbers, the mental effort required can help to block out intrusive thoughts and reduce worry. At the very least, it's impossible to panic about being awake when you are occupying your brain with a complicated or repetitive task.

★ COUNTER-PRODUCTIVE SHEEP ★

If you do choose to bore yourself to sleep, research by scientists at Oxford University's Department of Experimental Psychology indicates that counting sheep is a less effective method than other distraction techniques such as imagining a relaxing beach. In their study, which was published in the journal *Behaviour Research and Therapy*, insomniacs were instructed to distract themselves by several methods, including counting sheep and imagining a tranquil scene. 'Picturing an engaging scene takes up more brain space than the same dirty old sheep,' says researcher Allison Harvey. 'Plus it's easier to stay with it because it's more interesting.' On average, the sheep-counters took 20 minutes longer to get to sleep than their counterparts.

★ CHECK YOUR LEVELS OF POTASSIUM ★

Potassium helps to consolidate sleep efficiency and appears to reduce the amount of waking during the night. It has a role in regulating blood pressure and is important for the function of muscles, including the heart. Potassium deficiency causes fatigue, muscle cramps, tingling or numbness, constipation and palpitations. In a study from the University of California San Diego published in the journal *Sleep*, researchers found that potassium chloride supplements significantly increased sleep efficiency. Dietary sources of potassium include white beans, avocado, dark leafy greens like spinach, sweet potatoes, coconut water, bananas, baked potatoes with skins, dried apricots and yoghurt.

★ COMBINE MILK WITH CARBS ★

Some people include a mug of warm milk in their bedtime ritual to help them feel sleepy. Milk contains tryptophan, which is involved in the production of melatonin (which helps control your sleep and wake cycles). During the day it is important to eat foods that contain tryptophan (see page 5) but a glass of milk on its own before bed won't affect you biochemically unless combined with carbohydrate-rich food, otherwise the only benefit will be psychological.

★ YOGA POSE NO. 2 ★

Stand with your feet about six inches apart. Keeping your knees straight but not rigid, allow your upper torso to fold towards the ground, with your arms dangling. Keep your head loose and relaxed and allow your spine to lengthen each time you exhale. Don't force your hands to touch your toes, simply allow gravity to draw them closer to the ground as you exhale. Explore for three minutes, then gently curl back up again.

Sleep is God. Go worship.

JIM BUTCHER

★ CHECK YOUR LEVELS OF VITAMIN C ★

Vitamin C is very important for healthy restorative sleep. Studies published in recent years report that lack of vitamin C may cause shorter and non-restorative sleep. Researchers from the University of Pennsylvania reviewed data from the National Health and Nutrition Examination Survey and found that people who consumed lower levels of vitamin C slept for just five to six hours each night. Other studies have found a link between low blood levels of vitamin C and sleep disturbances, such as waking up during the night. Injections of vitamin C have even been shown to improve the sleep of people with sleep apnoea. In the UK, recommendations are 90mg for men and 75mg for women daily and in the US it is 60mg for adults. Dietary sources of vitamin C include bell peppers, dark green leafy vegetables, broccoli, kiwi fruit, oranges, strawberries, tomatoes, spinach and peas.

Sleeplessness is a desert without vegetation or inhabitants.

JESSAMYN WEST

Take rest; a field that has rested gives a bountiful crop.

OVID

★ INSTALL F.LUX ON YOUR COMPUTER/TABLET ★

F.lux is freeware that works in the background to control the colour temperature of your computer screen, like sunlight during the day and warmer at night, so that you don't get bombarded with sleep-wrecking blue light if you are working at a screen during the evening. Its website explains the concept with disarming clarity: 'During the day, computer screens look good – they're designed to look like the sun. But, at 9pm, 10pm, or 3am, you probably shouldn't be looking at the sun.' F.lux automatically warms up your computer's screen colours at sunset and returns them to normal at sunrise, to make your computer screen blend with the room you're in. You simply tell it what kind of lighting you have and where in the world you live, then you can forget about it. No more working into the evening and then taking hours to wind down.

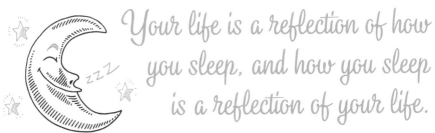

Your life is a reflection of how you sleep, and how you sleep is a reflection of your life.

DR RAFAEL PELAYO

★ CHECK YOUR LEVELS OF SELENIUM ★

Selenium is an essential trace mineral and antioxidant that is vital to good physical and mental energy as well as sleep. Selenium is important to one of the body's master antioxidants, glutathione peroxidase, which keeps cell membranes from becoming damaged by oxidisation. Chronic selenium deficiency causes heart problems and is thought to be a factor in gastrointestinal, liver and prostate cancers. Signs you may be selenium deficient include hair loss and discoloration of skin and fingernails (heavy whitening of the fingernail beds), low immunity and chronic fatigue. In the UK, recommendations are 75mcg for men and 60mcg for women daily and in the US it is 55mcg for adults. Dietary sources of selenium include brazil nuts (2 nuts a day is all you need), shrimp, sardines, salmon, tuna, shiitake mushrooms, broccoli, asparagus and spinach.

He tried counting Sheep, which is sometimes a good way of getting to sleep, and; as that was no good, he tried counting Heffalumps.

A. A. MILNE, *WINNIE-THE-POOH*

★ TAKE A COOL SHOWER JUST BEFORE BEDTIME ★

Your body temperature falls before you sleep, so give it a helping hand by having a cool (not cold) shower. Start with a warm shower and then reduce the temperature until the water is bearably cool (rather than freezing cold – the last thing you need is an adrenalin rush at this time in the evening). After a few minutes, dry yourself, brush your teeth and go straight to bed. You'll feel cool and fresh and ready for sleep.

Never go to sleep without a request to your subconscious.

THOMAS A. EDISON

★ ROCK-A-BYE ★

Everyone knows that babies like to be rocked to sleep, and who hasn't enjoyed a lazy afternoon dozing in a hammock? It is clear that there is a relationship between rocking and sleep, but that link is still poorly understood. So in 2011, researchers from the University of Geneva, Switzerland tested twelve healthy men (22–38 years old) aiming 'to demonstrate that swinging can modulate physiological parameters of human sleep'. Each subject took two 45-minute afternoon naps on a bed that was either gently rocking or stationary, while their brain activity was continually monitored. All the men fell asleep more quickly when the bed was rocking, they moved more quickly into the deeper stage N2 sleep (about 50 per cent of an adult's total sleep) and eight of them said they found the rocking nap more pleasant than the stationary one. So the next time sleep eludes you, imagine you're in a hammock, slowly being rocked from side to side by a cool breeze on a warm beach.

★ SKIP A FEW MEALS TO BEAT JET LEG ★

Drink plenty of water while long-haul travelling and avoid caffeine and alcohol. Your sleep cycle is as much linked to eating times as it is to light and dark, so when you land half a world away from home and your digestive system is twelve hours out of synch, skip some meals – fast for between 12 and 16 hours – to help reset your body's sleep–wake cycle.

★ ROLL YOUR EYES BACK ★

When you can't get to sleep, try rolling your eyes up in the direction of your forehead, while keeping them closed. It sends a message to your brain that you are ready to sleep. Now try rolling your eyes down in the direction of your nose. Both positions have a powerful effect on your consciousness. Make sure you keep your neck and shoulders relaxed during this experiment, and don't press your chin forward into your chest. Breathe deeply and enjoy the slightly disorienting feeling, then return your eyes to their normal relaxed position. Even if eye rolling doesn't send you off to sleep, your curiosity and attentiveness to this new experience will give you a welcome break from the repetitive and worrisome thoughts that might be the real cause of your insomnia.

Try to sleep.
Tomorrow's coming,
whether we worry
about it or not.

VERONICA ROSSI

I wasn't really asleep. I was just meditating on unconsciousness.

PAUL BOURGET

★ CHECK WHETHER MEDICATION IS RUINING YOUR SLEEP ★

If you take medication, ask your doctor how each drug affects your sleep. Beta blockers, which treat high blood pressure, heart problems, glaucoma and migraines, often decrease the amount of REM and slow-wave sleep, making you feel groggy during the day. Alpha blockers (used to treat high blood pressure and prostate problems) also affect REM sleep, causing daytime drowsiness. Antihistamines – often used to treat a number of allergic health conditions – cause drowsiness and antidepressants can wreak havoc with your sleeping habits, and cause insomnia in some people. Do not stop taking your medication without consulting your doctor, but make sure you are fully informed of its side-effects with respect to your sleeping patterns, so you know what to expect.

A little insomnia is not without its value in making us appreciate sleep, in throwing a ray of light upon that darkness.

MARCEL PROUST

★ TAKE ST. JOHN'S WORT ★

St. John's Wort is the perennial flowering plant *Hypericum perforatum*, native to many parts of Europe and the US. For centuries it has been widely used as a herbal remedy for insomnia and depression, weight loss and anxiety. You can buy it in tinctures (dissolved in alcohol), pills or in herbal teas. Many people report benefits in enhanced mood and sleep. The primary active ingredient is hyperforin which is believed to increase levels of dopamine, which is important for sleep regulation. Consult a doctor or pharmacist before using it as it can interfere with some types of medication, and as with any over-the-counter product, it should not be used as a substitute for prescribed medication or consulting your GP.

★ DON'T COMPROMISE YOUR SLEEP FOR ★ THE SAKE OF YOUR PARTNER

Partners can be a huge obstacle to a good night's sleep, whether it's differing comfort needs, stealing the duvet or loud snoring, or maybe you're in the early stages of a relationship and your partner insists on being cuddled all night, which you find uncomfortable. Whatever the issue, you both need quality undisturbed sleep, so it is imperative that you are honest with each other to find a solution that works for both of you, rather than tolerate years of impaired sleep. Duvet wars can be solved by having two single duvets and you can even buy double mattresses suitable for different requirements on each side. With snoring, it's the responsibility of the snorer to do everything possible to reduce the problem.

There are two kinds of people, those who like to sleep next to the wall, and those who like to sleep next to the people who push them off the bed.

ETGAR KERET

★ TRY TO COMBAT SNORING ★

Snoring occurs when air is obstructed as it passes through the nose and throat during sleep. The surrounding tissue in the head and neck vibrates, causing the distinctive rasping sound. There are several ways to reduce or even eliminate snoring. Overweight people tend to have more soft tissue around their throat and face, so the best solution is to lose excess weight, which not only reduces the obstruction, but also any possible inflammation. Dehydration also impedes air flow by narrowing passageways, so stay hydrated and avoid alcohol, which dehydrates and also abnormally relaxes the throat muscles and narrows airways. Snoring can be improved by sleeping on your side (when you lie on your back, neck fat presses down on your throat). Smoking also causes inflammation to your nose and throat, so it is another exacerbating factor.

Laugh and the world laughs with you; snore and you sleep alone.

ANTHONY BURGESS

Each night, when I go to sleep, I die. And the next morning, when I wake up, I am reborn.

MAHATMA GANDHI

★ PRESS HERE! NO. 3 ★

Locate acupressure point PC6 (the Inner Gate point), on the middle of the inside of your wrist, two finger widths from the palm. Press firmly with the thumb of your other hand for one minute, then perform the same on the other wrist.

I never liked sleeping; I always think I am missing something.

FRANCISCO COSTA

★ GET LOTS OF NATURAL SUNLIGHT ★

If you want better sleep, get more exposure to sunlight. Sunlight increases the release of the neurotransmitter serotonin in the body, which is associated with boosting mood and contributing to wellbeing and happiness. Serotonin also affects appetite and digestion, sexual desire and function, memory and – you guessed it – sleep. Recent research with a small sample of 49 office workers (27 in windowless workplaces and 22 in workplaces with windows) found that the workers who got more sunlight slept an average of 46 minutes more per night and were more physically active during the day. They were also happier and healthier than their troglodyte counterparts. Also, try to increase your exposure to early morning sunlight, within the first hour after waking, as this is linked to sounder sleep.

★ AVOID CAFFEINE ★

Everyone knows that coffee helps you to stay awake, but were you aware that a cup of coffee can reduce your sleep even when drunk over six hours before bedtime? The safest option is to drink your last coffee of the day no later than three o'clock in the afternoon. But coffee isn't the only culprit. A strong cup of tea contains as much caffeine as a weak cup of coffee, and many soft drinks have high levels. Energy drinks also contain caffeine. One 250ml can of Red Bull contains 80mg of caffeine, about the same as a cup of coffee. Also, caffeine is added to many over-the-counter cold and flu remedies as well as some versions of common painkillers such as paracetamol, ibuprofen and aspirin.

Sleep: a poor substitute for caffeine!

WALLY SHAWN

★ BAN PETS FROM THE BED OR BEDROOM ★ IF THEY AFFECT YOU SLEEP

Sharing your bed or bedroom with cats and dogs is a controversial but ultimately personal choice. A recent study of 23,000 dog owners found that more than half let their pets sleep on their beds. However, between 10 and 20 per cent of cat and dog owners report having their sleep disturbed by their pets. If it works for you, with no ill effects, don't change anything, because studies also show increased contentment and relaxation among pet owners who share their bed and enjoy enhanced sleep. But if a pet is disturbing you, make the necessary changes, because sleep should always be the highest priority.

Sleep is like a cat: it only comes to you if you ignore it.

GILLIAN FLYNN

The amount of sleep required by the average person is five minutes more.

WILSON MIZENER

★ LISTEN TO THE RAINFOREST OR A THUNDERSTORM ★

Many problem sleepers report the wonder of listening to one of the many rainforest relaxation tracks available on YouTube as they fall asleep. You really need to use headphones for a fully immersive experience. It can create a paradoxical state of alert relaxation, because on the one hand, sleeping in a rainforest makes many people feel disorientated, even scared, but you can enjoy the curious frisson of adventure as you luxuriate in the safety of your bed. A similar effect can be experienced by listening to a storm track, with the sporadic rumble of thunder and the crackle of lightning, accompanied by torrential rain.

Sleep that knits up the ravelled sleave of care
The death of each day's life, sore labour's bath
Balm of hurt minds, great nature's second course,
Chief nourisher in life's feast.

WILLIAM SHAKESPEARE, *MACBETH*

~~~~~~

★ WEAR LOOSE, COMFORTABLE NIGHTCLOTHES ★

If you must wear nightclothes (see page 20 for the benefits of sleeping naked) they should allow free body movement and should help to maintain a cool, sleep-friendly body temperature. Wear natural fabrics such as cotton or silk that allow your skin to breathe so that your body can perspire freely if necessary. Ideally, the room temperature and your bedding should keep your body cool, so if you do wake up sweating, remove some bedding or turn down the thermostat. During the winter, try to reach a comfortable temperature by investing in a top quality high-tog duvet (or an extra 6-tog add-on, or eiderdown) rather than layering up on clothing, because the fewer clothes you wear in bed, the better you will sleep.

★ USE EARPLUGS IF YOU CAN'T AVOID NOISE ★

If your environment has inescapable noise, consider using earplugs, ear muffs or headphones to help you drop off to sleep. Make sure you find earplugs that fit correctly, otherwise you could damage your ears. The best ones are custom made by a hearing healthcare professional, who will take an impression of your ear. It's an expensive option, but usually offers the best results. Disposable earplugs are made from soft foam, while mouldable ones are made of wax or silicone. Discontinue use if you develop headaches or if the pressure in your ear is uncomfortable.

I'm really good at sleeping on planes. I mean, I smell jet fuel and I'm out; I'm asleep for take-off.

ANTHONY BOURDAIN

★ CREATE A HOME FROM HOME ★

When you're sleeping away from home you may not be able to control your sleeping environment as fully as when you're tucked up in your own bed, but one thing you can usually take with you is your pillow. Not only will it maintain the correct head–neck posture while you sleep, but it will also make one piece of your surroundings familiar, which will help you to relax. The other major factors that you can control are the times you go to sleep and wake, which should be as close as possible to your normal domestic routine (if you don't have a routine, get one). Wherever possible, try to get the temperature right (18°C/65°F) – you can even travel with a thermometer to help you achieve the optimal sleeping temperature.

There is something in the New York air that makes sleep useless.

SIMONE DE BEAUVOIR

★ AVOID DEEP DISCUSSIONS AND ESPECIALLY ★ ARGUMENTS BEFORE BED

For two hours before bed you should be winding down, so it's obvious that a confrontation is the last thing you should be involved with if you want a good night's sleep. Of course, arguments can't always be avoided (especially when one party wants to park the beef until the morning to get some shut-eye). Adrenalin can take several hours to leave your system, so wherever possible, resist starting a sentence with the phrase 'We've got to talk' until after breakfast!

★ DON'T HIT SNOOZE ★

If you must use an alarm clock, don't hit the snooze button. It's bad enough being woken once, but drifting in and out of sleep, punctuated by an alarm every five minutes, plays havoc with your hormone levels and leaves you in a state of grogginess called 'sleep inertia'. It makes you feel as if getting out of bed is not your own decision, which is a very disempowering way to begin each day. Be decisive: get up as soon as the alarm goes off, so that it feels like your choice. If some mornings you wake up naturally at 5.30am or 6am and feel fine and functional, there's no harm in getting up and having some time to yourself before your busy day begins. If you feel all right, don't force yourself back to sleep just because habit tells you that 7am is 'normal'. You will benefit from having woken without an alarm clock, plus you get some extra free time before breakfast.

Sullen monosyllabism, a sure sign of sleep deprivation.

JIM BUTCHER

★ DO THE COGNITIVE SHUFFLE ★

When you're trying to sleep or get back to sleep, intrusive thoughts often overwhelm a racing mind. 'Cognitive shuffle' involves generating random ideas and images and then visualising them to block out unwanted thoughts and worries. 'It is actually very difficult for people to conjure up random images unaided,' says Luc Beaudoin, an adjunct professor in cognitive science and education at Simon Fraser University. Fortunately he's designed an app for that: mySleepButton generates and verbalises diverse random scenes and images and all you have to do is listen to the words and phrases and visualise them. You can set a timer so the voice doesn't run all night, and you can vary the time between each item. The app comes with a 'Simple Things' pack but you can purchase additional packs and languages.

★ DON'T JUST LIE THERE – GET UP AFTER 20 MINUTES ★

If you've been lying in bed for twenty minutes and you know that sleep isn't going to come any time soon, the panic has started to stir in your stomach and you're already starting to ruminate on a litany of chores and worries, get up. Get out of bed and don't lie down again until you feel sleepy. If you stay in bed and worry, you'll associate your bed with worrying. As soon as you accept that being awake is not the end of the world, you open up two choices: either to acknowledge your worries so that you can set them aside for eight hours while you sleep, or do something completely different and enjoyable to divert your attention away from your problems.

If you can't sleep, then get up and do something instead of lying there and worrying. It's the worry that gets you, not the loss of sleep.

DALE CARNEGIE

★ FLEX YOUR TOES ★

The Sleep Disorders Center at the University of Maryland Medical Center recommends toe tensing to aid sleep by drawing tension away from the rest of the body. Sometimes we hold on to tension by our hyper-awareness, in other words we try to force ourselves to relax when we should be doing nothing. Placing all your focus on one area allows the rest of the body to relax precisely because focus is taken away from it. Lie on your back with your eyes closed. Flex your ten toes back toward your knees. Count to 10 slowly. Now relax your toes. Count to 10 slowly. Repeat the flexing , relaxing and counting another nine times.

Sleep is death without the responsibility.

FRAN LEBOWITZ

O magic sleep! O comfortable bird,
That broodest o'er the troubled
sea of the mind
Till it is hush'd and smooth!

JOHN KEATS

★ AVOID HABITUAL SLEEPING IN ★

When you need to sleep in, you have a sleep debt, which means that your natural sleeping patterns have been disrupted. Sometimes we can't help this, because work or an event means we have to stay up later than normal. In this case, it's OK to lie in to reach your target seven to nine hours' sleep (although it's actually preferable to have a daytime nap to pay back a temporary sleep deficit). However, habitual sleeping in is abnormal. So if you regularly need to sleep in just to feel half functional, you need to focus instead on getting your sleeping pattern back to a consistent healthy norm.

There, in the depths of sleep, is the communion of the living and the dead.

GENNADY AYGI

★ CHECK YOUR LEVELS OF OMEGA-3 ★

Studies suggest that having higher levels of Omega-3 DHA is associated with better sleep. Researchers from the University of Oxford published results of their Omega-3 DHA sleep study in the *Journal of Sleep Research*. They studied 362 children from the UK between the ages of 7 and 9 years old and found that children who were given 600mg supplements of Omega-3 DHA slept for an hour longer each night and experienced fewer waking episodes than the children in the control group. Dietary sources of Omega-3s include krill oil, flaxseed oil, fish oil (salmon, sardine, cod liver, herring), chia seeds, walnuts, fish roe (caviar), oily fish (mackerel, salmon, herring, anchovy, tuna) soybeans and spinach.

★ WAKE UP NATURALLY ★

If you are woken every morning by your alarm clock, that should be a big warning sign that you are not getting enough sleep. An alarm clock literally disrupts your sleep – that's what it's designed to do. Millions of people are woken every day by an alarm clock but they never consider that this means it's impossible for them to enjoy optimal sleep. It's curious that you can be blind to this fact, and yet if the same interruption happened during your waking life, you'd know something was wrong. For example, you wouldn't tolerate having your plate taken away in the middle of a meal, or having the water switched off while you were taking a shower. Instead, simply go to bed earlier and wake naturally, feeling refreshed, in time to turn off the alarm before it buzzes.

To sleep is an act of faith.

BARBARA G. HARRISON

★ MODIFY YOUR HOME AND WORKPLACE ★

If you want better sleep, modify your home and workplace to get more exposure to sunlight. If you spend lots of time indoors, it's important to make sure your work and home environment are set up to allow the maximum amount of natural sunlight to enter. Trim bushes and trees directly outside your windows, but consider more extreme measures if large trees or hedges throw the whole house into shade. Keep windows clean and decorate with white and light colours, to bounce light around the rooms. Open your curtains and blinds as wide as they will go. Hang some large mirrors, to reflect light and to make the space seem bigger. At work, try to position your desk near a window. If you have little control over the workspace, ask your employer to use natural light bulbs or invest in a light therapy lamp and explain to your boss that it will improve your productivity.

When I'm sleeping I do a lot of living.

DAVID JOHANSEN

I have no trouble sleeping.

DALAI LAMA

★ USE A LIGHT THERAPY LAMP ★

If your mood suffers during the winter months because you aren't getting enough sunlight, this will also affect your sleep. Use a light therapy lamp, which emits very bright light that mimics natural outdoor light to boost your levels of serotonin. The lamp should offer the full spectrum of bright white light but not include harmful ultraviolet rays. A light therapy lamp will stimulate serotonin release if it emits light to a minimum of 2,500 lux, but for best results, use 10,000 lux (this is 20 times the strength of ordinary indoor lighting). Place the lamp in your peripheral vision at eye level or higher about two feet away (you don't stare at it directly). Only use it in the morning, especially if it emits blue light. Used daily, your mood should improve within two or three weeks and you will also enjoy better sleep.

I like sleeping **a lot.**

IAN MCKELLEN

★ DRINK LEMON BALM TEA ★

Lemon balm is an ancient perennial herb from the mint family that has been used for centuries to treat digestive problems, lift mood, promote wellbeing and aid sleep. It has scientifically proven sedative properties (its most important active ingredient appears to be rosmarinic acid, as well as the complex interaction between its several dozen chemical components).

Recipe

Place two tablespoons each of dried lemon balm and dried chamomile into a mug, along with one teaspoon of honey.
Fill the mug with boiling water, stir and then allow to brew for five minutes. Strain and drink 45 minutes before bedtime.

Prolonged use is not recommended, but a lemon-scented nightcap once a week is safe. Lemon balm may lower your blood pressure and blood sugar levels, so consult your doctor before use if you are on medication.

I love to sleep. Do you? Isn't it great? It really is the best of both worlds. You get to be alive and unconscious.

RITA RUDNER

★ HIDE YOUR ALARM CLOCK ★

Turn the face away from you, because when you're struggling to get to sleep, it reduces the temptation to clock watch, which not only increases your stress levels, but also shines wakeful light into your eyes (especially if you use a mobile phone to check the time). It also stops you checking the time when you wake up during the night. It's normal to wake up several times during the night, but if you fixate on checking the time, you're just inviting your brain to start calculating how long you've been asleep or how many hours you have left until you have to get up. This is not conducive to healthy sleep! Also, checking the clock may even increase the likelihood of you waking up at the same time tomorrow night – a cheeky glance at the clock can quickly turn into an excruciating nightly routine.

When is the night over? Is it the start of sunrise or the end of it? Is it when you finally go to sleep or simply when you realise that you have to?

RACHEL COHN

Think in the morning.

Act in the noon. Eat in the evening. Sleep in the night.

WILLIAM BLAKE

★ SET AN ALARM TO GO TO BED ★

Setting an alarm to tell you it's time to go to bed is much better for your health than being woken by an alarm every morning. You obey the morning alarm because you know that your present and future livelihood or the wellbeing of your family depends on you getting up and having a productive day. But the things that matter to you are even more dependent on you getting a good night's sleep. If you obey the alarm in the evening, within a week you won't need one to wake you in the morning.

Eat healthily, sleep well, breathe deeply, move harmoniously.

JEAN-PIERRE BARRAL

★ EAT IN MODERATION DURING THE EARLY EVENING ★

When you go to bed you should feel neither stuffed nor hungry. Night-time should be an opportunity for your mind and body to be refreshed and repaired but you can only gain the maximum benefit once the digestion of your evening meal is complete. Some people make it a rule never to eat after six o'clock. There is evidence that the body benefits from an overnight fasting period of at least twelve hours, but if you wake during the night feeling hungry, push that final meal slightly later. Evidence also suggests that eating more calories later in the evening is associated with obesity. Some nutritionists encourage the old adage 'breakfast like a king, lunch like a prince and dine like a pauper'. Whatever regime you choose, never skip meals, because your body needs a reliable source of energy throughout the day.

Sit comfortably with both feet flat on the floor. Lift your left foot and place it on your right knee. Locate the slight indent between your big toe and second toe. Press firmly with your right thumb for one minute while keeping your eyes closed and breathing deeply. Release for thirty seconds. Repeat twice, then switch legs.

The only thing that I'm obsessed with is sleeping, and actually, it is more than an obsession, it is a pleasure.

CHRISTIAN BALE

★ BECOME MORE PHYSICALLY ACTIVE ★

Regular exercise improves heart health and blood pressure, builds muscle and bone, reduces stress and is a mood booster, all of which contribute to better sleep. It also helps to regulate the hormones which control the cycle of waking and sleep. There are surprisingly few studies into the effect of exercise on chronic insomnia, but the limited evidence suggests that it has a significant positive effect and that moderate-intensity aerobic exercise (e.g. walking) is preferable to vigorous aerobic exercise or lifting weights. Make sure you finish exercising at least two hours before bedtime, to allow your body to cool down and for adrenalin levels to fall.

There are twelve hours in the day, and above fifty in the night.

MARIE DE RABUTIN-CHANTAL

Care keeps his watch in every old man's eye,
And where care lodges, sleep will never lie.

WILLIAM SHAKESPEARE, *ROMEO AND JULIET*

★ KEEP A SLEEP DIARY ★

Keeping a sleep diary is a great way to learn about the factors in your daily life that impact your sleep. Record the time you went to bed and woke up; whether you awoke naturally or to an alarm; how rested you felt on waking. Include how many times you got up during the night and things that hampered sleep (hunger, overeating, temperature, pain, noise, light, worrying thoughts, health issues, etc.). Use the diary to monitor energy levels during the day, your mood, meals and exercise, how much caffeine and alcohol you consume, external stressors, drugs and medication and anything else that you feel is relevant. Over the coming weeks, as you build up a detailed picture of your waking and sleeping experiences, you will come to appreciate more than ever before the importance of making quality sleep a major priority.

★ YOGA POSE NO. 3 ★

Kneel on the floor, then place your palms flat on the floor so you form a 'table', with your back as the top and your head and neck in line with your back. Your knees should be directly below your hips and your straight arms perpendicular to the floor. As you exhale, arch your back towards the ceiling and relax your head; as you inhale return to the table-top position. Repeat several times while maintaining slow, deep, even breathing.

★ USE SLEEP-INDUCING ESSENTIAL OILS ★

Dozens of essential oils are associated with relaxation and sleep, from the familiar lavender, chamomile, valerian, orange and frankincense to the lesser-known vetiver, ylang ylang, sweet marjoram and bergamot. You can rub a few drops on the back of your neck before bedtime (diluted in a plain carrier oil), use an essential oil diffuser, spray onto your pillow with a water spritzer or add several drops to your bath. Experiment with a wide range of oils and oil blends because in the end, it's all a matter of personal preference.

Sleep is the best meditation.

DALAI LAMA

The feeling of sleepiness when you are not in bed, and can't get there, is the meanest feeling in the world.

EDGAR WATSON HOWE

★ TRY TO STAY AWAKE ★

Imagine you're back at school during the last lesson on a Friday afternoon and all you want to do is go to sleep, so you put your elbows on your desk and cup your hands over your eyebrows so you can close your eyes for a few moments without the teacher seeing. Remember how all-consuming was your desire to sleep, because you weren't allowed? You can create a similar effect in bed with reverse psychology by opening your eyes wide and telling yourself that you must stay awake. Your eye muscles will quickly tire and start sending messages to your brain that it's time to sleep. Keep resisting and take a few deep breaths. Fight the urge to close your eyes until you reach a point where you sense that you are ready to fall asleep.

The last refuge of the insomniac is a sense of superiority to the sleeping world.

LEONARD COHEN

★ USE STEP-BY-STEP MUSCLE RELAXATION ★

This is a widely known relaxation technique, but don't knock it until you've tried it. Lie on your back and focus on your breathing. Place the heel of one hand on your chest bone and apply firm pressure with both hands as you make small clockwise circles. This will help to release tension in your chest and encourage you to breathe from your abdomen. Then place your hands by your sides, take a deep breath, tense your toes and feet for about five seconds, and then release as you breathe out. Breathe in and tense your calves for about five seconds, then release as you breathe out. Work your way up your body, symmetrically tensing and relaxing specific body areas – hands, lower arms, then upper arms, shoulders and neck – until it is the turn of your face. Finally tense and relax your whole body three times, then return to stillness and listen to the sound of your breathing.

★ CHECK YOUR LEVELS OF VITAMINS B6 AND B12 ★

Vitamin B6 is important for healthy sleep because it is vital in the body's metabolism of tryptophan and serotonin. Vitamin B12 deficiency has been linked to an abnormal sleep–wake rhythm. One of the best ways to boost your serotonin levels is to consume foods that contain vitamin B6, which include sunflower seeds, pistachio nuts, fish (tuna, wild salmon), turkey, chicken, lean pork, dried prunes, lean beef, sweet potato, bananas and avocados. Vitamin B6 deficiency can be caused by excess consumption of alcohol or sugary and processed foods. Vitamin B6 deficiency symptoms include skin inflammation, depression, anaemia, low energy and impaired mental performance. Dietary sources of vitamin B12 include shellfish, liver, oily fish (mackerel, salmon, herring, tuna), crab, crayfish, fortified cereals and soy products and red meat.

O sleep, O gentle sleep,
Nature's soft nurse, how have I frighted thee,
That thou no more wilt weigh my eyelids down
And steep my sense in forgetfulness?

WILLIAM SHAKESPEARE, *HENRY IV, PART I*

★ REDUCE LONG DAYTIME NAPS ★

Although napping is seen as a common age-related occurrence, there is little research about its benefits or consequences. If you enjoy long daytime naps and you have no problem sleeping at night, there's no need to alter your routine. However, if you struggle to sleep at night, your daytime napping could be partly to blame. In general, short 'power' naps of between 10 and 25 minutes have been proved to be beneficial, increasing alertness and wellbeing. Longer naps – especially in the afternoon and evening – can cause sleep problems by confusing your body clock. If you have difficulty sleeping at night, restrict your nap to 20 minutes in the early afternoon, or preferably eliminate completely.

Daytime sleep is like the sin of the flesh; the more you have the more you want, and yet you feel unhappy, sated and unsated at the same time.

UMBERTO ECO

There is nothing so entirely
desirable in all the world
as a few hours' oblivion.

ANNE REEVE ALDRICH

⋆ BREATHE THROUGH ALTERNATE NOSTRILS ⋆

This calming yoga technique is called *nadi shodhana*. Sit comfortably
with your back straight (but not rigid) and become aware of your
breathing as you quieten your mind and listen to the sound of the breath
flowing in and out of your body. After observing this for a while, use your
right hand to control the flow of breath, without disrupting its gentle
regular rhythm. Close off the left nostril with the index finger of your
right hand and breathe in. Then release the left nostril as you close off
the right nostril with the right thumb and breathe out. Then, with your
thumb still in place, breathe in through the left nostril, then close the left
and breathe out through the right. Repeat this cycle for several minutes.

DIVE INTO A BOWL OF ICY WATER *

Fill a sink with cold water, add ice cubes and then immerse your face in it for thirty seconds. This triggers a phenomenon known as the mammalian dive reflex, which immediately slows down your heart rate and diverts blood away from the peripheries (e.g. limbs) to feed vital organs such as the heart and brain. This is called peripheral vasoconstriction and it reduces the body's oxygen requirement so mammals can stay underwater for longer. After you surface you will feel calmer and your blood pressure will be lower.

Don't try to solve serious matters in the middle of the night.

PHILIP K. DICK

Did you sleep well? No, I made a couple of mistakes.

STEVEN WRIGHT

★ BLOW BUBBLES ★

Blowing bubbles is such a simple childish pleasure, but it can also be a powerful mindfulness tool that can help you to relax and sleep. Have you ever tried to blow bubbles and worry about something else at the same time? It's virtually impossible – that's because they are captivating in their beauty, fragility and transience and they encourage us to live in the moment, watching each bubble as it travels through the air. When one bursts, we immediately transfer our attention to another. There's just no room for other thoughts. Meanwhile, we produce the bubbles by deep, sustained breathing: we take a deep breath in and then exhale a very controlled stream of air. It's practically meditation!

The old idea of a composer suddenly having a terrific idea and sitting up all night to write it is nonsense. Night-time is for sleeping.

BENJAMIN BRITTEN

★ LISTEN TO WHITE NOISE ★

Some people benefit from listening to 'white noise' to help them fall asleep. Others find it a total hindrance, so give it a try but don't torture yourself if you decide that it isn't for you. White noise is consistent noise that comes out evenly across all audible frequencies and it helps to mask the many other little nocturnal sounds that might distract a light sleeper. Search for 'white noise' on YouTube. You could also try 'pink noise' (white noise with the higher frequencies turned down), 'violet noise' (aka purple noise or differentiated white noise, where the power density increases 6 dB per octave with increasing frequency – it sounds a bit like rainfall) or 'red noise' (where the power density decreases 6 dB per octave with increasing frequency – it sounds like a waterfall).

★ LISTEN TO A TALKING BOOK OR PODCAST ★

If you find dropping off to sleep a long haul, try listening to a talking book or podcast, which will distract you from the tedium, just as it can ease the monotony of a long car journey. It stops you focusing on the destination and allows you to live in the moment. What's the harm in lying in the darkness being entertained? It takes away the sense of urgency about getting to sleep and lets you feel you're doing something worthwhile with your time, rather than counting down the requisite forty minutes of tedium it normally takes you to fall asleep.

Sleep is that golden chain that ties health and our bodies together.

THOMAS DEKKER

★ PRESS HERE! NO. 5 ★

Locate acupressure point gallbladder 20 (GB20), the two hollows where the neck muscles meet the base of your skull. Press with both thumbs and massage the area with a small circular motion for 90 seconds (your right thumb moves clockwise, your left thumb anti-clockwise). It is a great treatment for the tension headaches and neck problems which can inhibit sleep.

From reading too much, and sleeping too little, his brain dried up on him and he lost his judgement.

MIGUEL DE CERVANTES